WOULD YOU RATHER

ADULT VERSION

FOLLOW US AT:

f **WWW.FACEBOOK.COM/ WOULDYOURATHERBOOK** **f**

⟨⊙⟩ **@WOULDYOURATHERBOOK** ⟨⊙⟩

WWW.WOULDYOURATHERBOOK.COM

Copyright ©Would You Rather ADULT VERSION
All rights reserved. This book or any portion thereof may not be
reproduced or used in any manner whatsoever
without the express written permission.

COME
JOIN OUR GROUP

GET A BONUS PDF PACKED WITH HILARIOUS JOKES, AND THINGS TO MAKE YOU SMILE!

GO TO:

shorturl.at/cdLRT

■ *Get a Bonus fun PDF* (filled with jokes, and fun would you rather questions)

■ *Get entered into our monthly competition to win a $100 Amazon gift card*

■ *Hear about our up and coming new books*

HOW TO PLAY?

You can play to win or play for fun, the choice is yours!

1. Player 1 asks player 2 to either choose questions **A** or **B**.

2. Then player 1 reads out the chosen questions.

3. Player 2 decides on an answer to their dilemma, and either memorize their answer or notes it down.

4. Player 1 has to guess player 2's answer. If they guess correctly they win a point, if not player 2 wins a point.

5. Take turns asking the questions, **the first to 7 points wins.**

REMEMBER
IF YOU CHOOSE TO ATTEMPT TO DO ANY OF THE SCENARIOS IN THIS BOOK, YOU DO SO AT YOUR OWN RISK

WOULD YOU RATHER?

ADULT
VERSION

PLAYER 1

(ASK THE OTHER PLAYER(S) TO
CHOOSE QUESTION A OR QUESTION B)

A WOULD YOU RATHER

HAVE THE CHANCE TO HAVE SEX IN A CAR

 OR

IN A TENT?

B WOULD YOU RATHER

HAVE SEX FIRST THING IN THE MORNING

 OR

LAST THING AT NIGHT?

WOULD YOU RATHER ?
ADULT
VERSION

PLAYER 2

(ASK THE OTHER PLAYER(S) TO
CHOOSE QUESTION A OR QUESTION B)

A WOULD YOU RATHER

WATCH PORN WITH YOUR PARTNER

TALK DIRTY?

B WOULD YOU RATHER

FOREPLAY

ROLE PLAY?

WOULD YOU RATHER ?
ADULT
VERSION

PLAYER 1

(ASK THE OTHER PLAYER(S) TO
CHOOSE QUESTION A OR QUESTION B)

A **WOULD YOU RATHER**

HAVE SEX AT NIGHT WITH THE LIGHTS TURNED ON

OFF?

B **WOULD YOU RATHER**

HAVE ONE PARTNER FOR THE REST OF YOUR LIFE

MULTIPLE PARTNERS?

WOULD YOU RATHER ?

ADULT
VERSION

PLAYER 2

(ASK THE OTHER PLAYER(S) TO
CHOOSE QUESTION A OR QUESTION B)

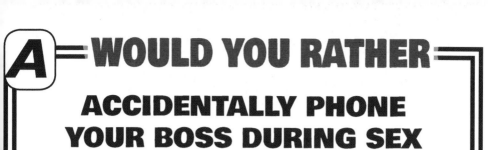

A — WOULD YOU RATHER

ACCIDENTALLY PHONE YOUR BOSS DURING SEX

 OR

YOUR MOTHER?

B — WOULD YOU RATHER

HAVE TO PAY FOR SEX

 OR

BE PAID FOR SEX?

WOULD YOU RATHER ?

ADULT
VERSION

PLAYER 1

(ASK THE OTHER PLAYER(S) TO
CHOOSE QUESTION A OR QUESTION B)

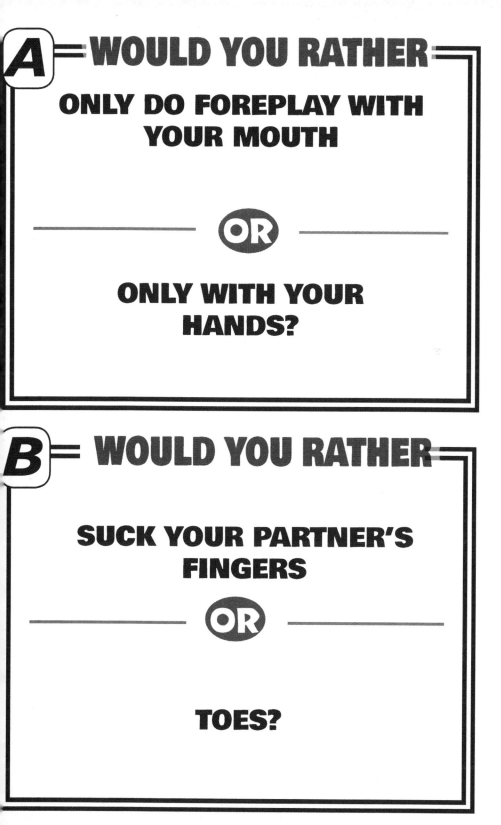

A **WOULD YOU RATHER**

ONLY DO FOREPLAY WITH YOUR MOUTH

OR

ONLY WITH YOUR HANDS?

B **WOULD YOU RATHER**

SUCK YOUR PARTNER'S FINGERS

OR

TOES?

WOULD YOU RATHER ?

ADULT
VERSION

PLAYER 2

(ASK THE OTHER PLAYER(S) TO
CHOOSE QUESTION A OR QUESTION B)

A — WOULD YOU RATHER

ONLY HAVE SEX IN THE MISSIONARY POSITION

 OR

DOGGY STYLE?

B — WOULD YOU RATHER

HAVE AMAZING SEX THAT IS OVER IN A MINUTE

 OR

AVERAGE SEX THAT LASTS FOR TEN MINUTES?

WOULD YOU RATHER?
ADULT
VERSION

PLAYER 1

(ASK THE OTHER PLAYER(S) TO
CHOOSE QUESTION A OR QUESTION B)

A **WOULD YOU RATHER**

HAVE BAD SEX WITH SOMEONE BEAUTIFUL

 OR

AMAZING SEX WITH SOMEONE YOU ARE NOT ATTRACTED TO?

B **WOULD YOU RATHER**

HAVE SHOWER SEX

 OR

FLOOR SEX?

WOULD YOU RATHER ?
ADULT
VERSION

PLAYER 2

(ASK THE OTHER PLAYER(S) TO
CHOOSE QUESTION A OR QUESTION B)

A | WOULD YOU RATHER

HAVE SEX WITH LOUD MUSIC

 OR

HAVE SEX IN COMPLETE SILENCE?

B | WOULD YOU RATHER

HAVE DRUNK SEX

 OR

HUNGOVER SEX?

WOULD YOU RATHER ?
ADULT
VERSION

PLAYER 1

(ASK THE OTHER PLAYER(S) TO
CHOOSE QUESTION A OR QUESTION B)

SPIT

 OR

SWALLOW?

HOOK UP IN THE BACK OF A CAR

 OR

THE BACK OF A CINEMA?

WOULD YOU RATHER ?
ADULT
VERSION

PLAYER 2

(ASK THE OTHER PLAYER(S) TO
CHOOSE QUESTION A OR QUESTION B)

A — WOULD YOU RATHER

GET A MASSAGE

 OR

CUDDLE UP IN FRONT OF A FIRE?

B — WOULD YOU RATHER

HAVE BAD ORAL SEX

 OR

NO ORAL SEX?

WOULD YOU RATHER ?
ADULT
VERSION

PLAYER 1

(ASK THE OTHER PLAYER(S) TO
CHOOSE QUESTION A OR QUESTION B)

A = WOULD YOU RATHER

DO IT IN THE COLD

 OR

DO IT WHEN IT'S HOT?

B = WOULD YOU RATHER

USE HOT CANDLE WAX DURING SEX

 OR

ICE CUBES?

WOULD YOU RATHER ?
ADULT
VERSION

PLAYER 2

(ASK THE OTHER PLAYER(S) TO
CHOOSE QUESTION A OR QUESTION B)

A = WOULD YOU RATHER

EAT FOOD OFF YOUR SIGNIFICANT OTHER

OR

HAVE THEM EAT FOOD OFF YOU?

B = WOULD YOU RATHER

BATH TOGETHER

OR

SHOWER TOGETHER?

WOULD YOU RATHER ?
ADULT
VERSION

PLAYER 1

(ASK THE OTHER PLAYER(S) TO
CHOOSE QUESTION A OR QUESTION B)

A — WOULD YOUR RATHER

HAVE QUICK SEX

 OR

WAIT TILL YOU HAVE MORE TIME?

B — WOULD YOU RATHER

HAVE SEX WITH SOMEONE A LOT SHORTER THAN YOU

 OR

A LOT TALLER THAN YOU?

WOULD YOU RATHER ?

ADULT
VERSION

PLAYER 2

(ASK THE OTHER PLAYER(S) TO
CHOOSE QUESTION A OR QUESTION B)

A WOULD YOU RATHER

BE ON TOP

 OR

ON THE BOTTOM?

B WOULD YOU RATHER

BE IN CONTROL

 **OR**

TOLD WHAT TO DO?

WOULD YOU RATHER ?

ADULT
VERSION

PLAYER 1

(ASK THE OTHER PLAYER(S) TO
CHOOSE QUESTION A OR QUESTION B)

A  WOULD YOU RATHER

BE SPANKED

 OR

GET CHOKED?

B WOULD YOU RATHER

HAVE A SMALL PENIS BUT KNOW WHAT TO DO WITH IT

 OR

A LARGE PENIS BUT BE USELESS WITH IT?

WOULD YOU RATHER?
ADULT
VERSION

PLAYER 2

(ASK THE OTHER PLAYER(S) TO
CHOOSE QUESTION A OR QUESTION B)

A WOULD YOU RATHER

HAVE SEX IN AN ABANDONED BUILDING

 OR

IN A FOREST AT NIGHT?

B WOULD YOU RATHER

SATISFY ANOTHER PERSON

 OR

BE SATISFIED?

WOULD YOU RATHER?

ADULT
VERSION

PLAYER 1

(ASK THE OTHER PLAYER(S) TO
CHOOSE QUESTION A OR QUESTION B)

A

WOULD YOU RATHER

YOUR NEIGHBORS HEAR YOU HAVING SEX

 OR

A STRANGER WALKS PAST AND SPOTS YOU HAVING SEX?

B

WOULD YOU RATHER

SKINNY DIP IN THE OCEAN WITH SOMEONE

 OR

HAVE A NAKED JACUZZI WITH THEM?

WOULD YOU RATHER ?

ADULT
VERSION

PLAYER 2

(ASK THE OTHER PLAYER(S) TO
CHOOSE QUESTION A OR QUESTION B)

A — WOULD YOU RATHER

BE UNDRESSED

 OR

UNDRESS SOMEONE ELSE?

B — WOULD YOU RATHER

TALK DIRTY ON A WEBCAM

 OR

OVER THE PHONE?

WOULD YOU RATHER ?

ADULT
VERSION

PLAYER 1

(ASK THE OTHER PLAYER(S) TO
CHOOSE QUESTION A OR QUESTION B)

A = WOULD YOU RATHER

WALK I ON YOUR MOM NAKED

 OR

HAVE YOUR MOM WALK IN ON YOU NAKED?

B = WOULD YOU RATHER

GIVE UP SEX FOR A YEAR

 OR

GIVE UP MASTURBATION FOR A YEAR?

WOULD YOU RATHER ?
ADULT
VERSION

PLAYER 2

(ASK THE OTHER PLAYER(S) TO
CHOOSE QUESTION A OR QUESTION B)

A  WOULD YOU RATHER

HAVE A NAKED PHOTO OF CIRCULATED ON THE INTERNET

 OR

APPEAR NAKED ON A WORK VIDEO CHAT?

B WOULD YOU RATHER

ACCIDENTALLY SAY "I LOVE YOU" TO YOUR BOSS

 OR

HAVE YOUR MOM OVERHEAR YOU TALKING DIRTY ON THE PHONE?

WOULD YOU RATHER ?

ADULT
VERSION

PLAYER 1

(ASK THE OTHER PLAYER(S) TO
CHOOSE QUESTION A OR QUESTION B)

A | WOULD YOU RATHER

HAVE SEX ON A PLANE

 OR

ON A TRAIN?

B | WOULD YOU RATHER

GET TOLD WHAT YOU ARE DOING WRONG IN BED

 OR

CARRY ON AS YOU WERE, NEVER KNOWING YOUR MISTAKES?

WOULD YOU RATHER ?
ADULT
VERSION

PLAYER 2

(ASK THE OTHER PLAYER(S) TO
CHOOSE QUESTION A OR QUESTION B)

A = WOULD YOU RATHER

HAVE THE BEST SEX OF YOUR LIFE WITH SOMEONE YOU'LL NEVER SEE AGAIN

 OR

HAVE BAD SEX ON TAP?

B = WOULD YOU RATHER

SEND NUDES TO AN EX

 OR

SEND NUDES TO A STRANGER?

WOULD YOU RATHER?
ADULT
VERSION

PLAYER 1

(ASK THE OTHER PLAYER(S) TO
CHOOSE QUESTION A OR QUESTION B)

A — WOULD YOU RATHER

WATCH A LAP DANCE

 OR

WATCH A STRIPPER?

B — WOULD YOU RATHER

HAVE TO WATCH YOUR PARENTS HAVE SEX

 OR

HAVE YOUR PARENTS WATCH YOU HAVE SEX?

WOULD YOU RATHER ?
ADULT
VERSION

PLAYER 2

(ASK THE OTHER PLAYER(S) TO
CHOOSE QUESTION A OR QUESTION B)

A WOULD YOU RATHER

HAVE AN ABNORMALLY HIGH SEX DRIVE

 OR

HAVE GROUP SEX WITH STRANGERS WITH PEOPLE YOU KNOW?

B WOULD YOU RATHER

GET INTERRUPTED DURING SEX BY SOMEONE WALKING IN

 OR

YOUR DOG LICKING YOUR FEET?

WOULD YOU RATHER ?

ADULT
VERSION

PLAYER 1

(ASK THE OTHER PLAYER(S) TO
CHOOSE QUESTION A OR QUESTION B)

A — WOULD YOU RATHER

HAVE SEX WITH A TREE

OR

NEVER HAVE SEX AGAIN?

B — WOULD YOU RATHER

HAVE ROMANTIC SEX

OR

ROUGH SEX?

WOULD YOU RATHER ?

ADULT
VERSION

PLAYER 2

(ASK THE OTHER PLAYER(S) TO
CHOOSE QUESTION A OR QUESTION B)

A = WOULD YOU RATHER

YOUR PARENTS KNEW WHEN YOU WERE HAVING SEX

 OR

YOU KNEW WHEN THEY WERE HAVING SEX?

B = WOULD YOU RATHER

UNDRESS SOMEONE ELSE

 OR

BE UNDRESSED?

WOULD YOU RATHER ?

ADULT
VERSION

PLAYER 1

(ASK THE OTHER PLAYER(S) TO
CHOOSE QUESTION A OR QUESTION B)

A WOULD YOU RATHER

BE SCRATCHED

 OR

TICKLED DURING SEX?

B WOULD YOU RATHER

ONLY SLEEP WITH PROSTITUTES

 OR

DIE A VIRGIN?

WOULD YOU RATHER ?

ADULT
VERSION

PLAYER 2

(ASK THE OTHER PLAYER(S) TO
CHOOSE QUESTION A OR QUESTION B)

A | WOULD YOU RATHER

FIND OUT THAT YOUR EX IS NOW SLEEPING WITH ONE OF YOUR PARENTS

OR

FIND OUT THAT YOUR CURRENT PARTNER USED TO SLEEP WITH ONE OF YOUR PARENTS?

B | WOULD YOU RATHER

HAVE LOTS OF SMALL ORGASMS

OR

ONE MASSIVE ONE?

WOULD YOU RATHER ?

ADULT
VERSION

PLAYER 1

(ASK THE OTHER PLAYER(S) TO
CHOOSE QUESTION A OR QUESTION B)

A  WOULD YOU RATHER

BE WITH SOMEONE WHO WALKS AROUND NAKED

 OR

WEARS SEXY OUTFITS?

B WOULD YOU RATHER

SLEEP WITH YOUR PARENT'S BEST FRIEND

 OR

YOUR BEST FRIEND'S PARENT?

WOULD YOU RATHER ?

ADULT
VERSION

PLAYER 2

(ASK THE OTHER PLAYER(S) TO
CHOOSE QUESTION A OR QUESTION B)

A | WOULD YOU RATHER

BE GOOD AT PICKING UP PEOPLE

OR

SOMEONE OTHERS TRY TO PICK UP?

B | WOULD YOU RATHER

A SEX TAPE OF YOU WAS LEAKED

OR

A VIDEO OF YOU MASTURBATING?

WOULD YOU RATHER ?
ADULT
VERSION

PLAYER 1

(ASK THE OTHER PLAYER(S) TO
CHOOSE QUESTION A OR QUESTION B)

A — WOULD YOU RATHER

FART WHEN YOU ORGASM

 OR

CRY WHEN YOU ORGASM?

B — WOULD YOU RATHER

DATE A PORN STAR

 OR

BE A PORN STAR?

WOULD YOU RATHER ?

ADULT
VERSION

PLAYER 2

(ASK THE OTHER PLAYER(S) TO
CHOOSE QUESTION A OR QUESTION B)

A | WOULD YOU RATHER

BE GOOD AT KISSING

 OR

GOOD AT ORAL SEX?

B | WOULD YOU RATHER

HAVE SEX WITH YOUR HIGH SCHOOL CRUSH

 OR

WITH YOUR CELEBRITY CRUSH?

WOULD YOU RATHER ?
ADULT
VERSION

PLAYER 1

(ASK THE OTHER PLAYER(S) TO
CHOOSE QUESTION A OR QUESTION B)

A  WOULD YOU RATHER

HAVE SEX WITH SOMEONE WHO IS CLEAN-SHAVEN

HAIRY?

B WOULD YOU RATHER

BE A VIRGIN TILL YOU TURN FORTY

NOT BE ABLE TO HAVE SEX AFTER FORTY:?

WOULD YOU RATHER ?

ADULT
VERSION

PLAYER 2

(ASK THE OTHER PLAYER(S) TO
CHOOSE QUESTION A OR QUESTION B)

A WOULD YOU RATHER

HAVE TO WEAR A BLINDFOLD

 OR

BE HANDCUFFED DURING SEX?

B WOULD YOU RATHER

DATE A SEX ADDICT

 OR

A VIRGIN?

WOULD YOU RATHER ?

ADULT
VERSION

PLAYER 1

(ASK THE OTHER PLAYER(S) TO
CHOOSE QUESTION A OR QUESTION B)

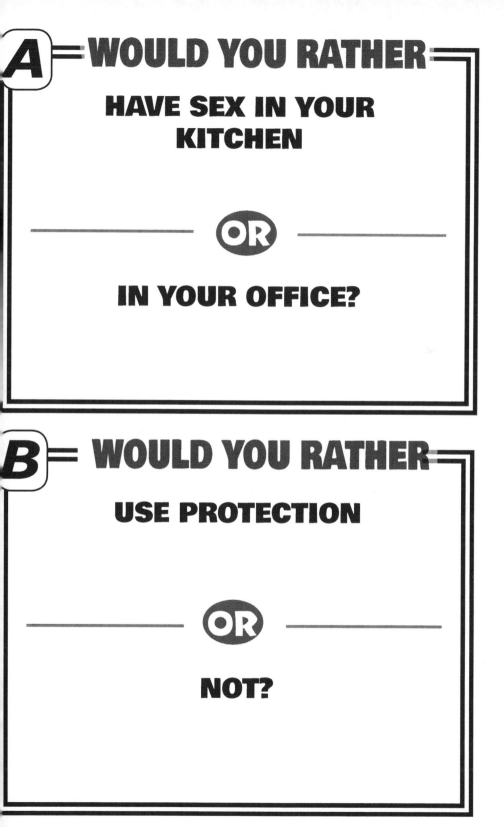

WOULD YOU RATHER ?

ADULT
VERSION

PLAYER 2

(ASK THE OTHER PLAYER(S) TO
CHOOSE QUESTION A OR QUESTION B)

A  WOULD YOU RATHER

**END A ONE NIGHT STAND
WITH AN INCURABLE STD**

 OR

EXPECTING A BABY?

B = WOULD YOU RATHER

**LOSE YOUR VIRGINITY TO
SOMEONE EXPERIENCED**

 OR

ANOTHER VIRGIN?

WOULD YOU RATHER ?

ADULT
VERSION

PLAYER 1

(ASK THE OTHER PLAYER(S) TO
CHOOSE QUESTION A OR QUESTION B)

A — WOULD YOU RATHER

GET CAUGHT HAVING SEX IN PUBLIC

 OR

MASTURBATING IN PUBLIC?

B — WOULD YOU RATHER

YOUR ONE NIGHT STAND LEAVES RIGHT AFTERWARD

 OR

IN THE MORNING?

WOULD YOU RATHER ?

ADULT
VERSION

PLAYER 2

(ASK THE OTHER PLAYER(S) TO
CHOOSE QUESTION A OR QUESTION B)

A = WOULD YOU RATHER

WATCH YOUR PARTNER TOUCH THEMSELVES

 OR

TOUCH YOURSELF IN FRONT OF THEM?

B = WOULD YOU RATHER

BE TIED UP

 OR

TIE SOMEONE ELSE UP?

WOULD YOU RATHER ?
ADULT
VERSION

PLAYER 1

(ASK THE OTHER PLAYER(S) TO
CHOOSE QUESTION A OR QUESTION B)

A WOULD YOU RATHER

HAVE FOREPLAY WITHOUT SEX

 OR

SEX WITHOUT FOREPLAY?

B WOULD YOU RATHER

HAVE SEX ON THE BONNET OF A CAR

 OR

IN THE BACKSEAT OF A CAR?

WOULD YOU RATHER?

ADULT
VERSION

PLAYER 2

(ASK THE OTHER PLAYER(S) TO
CHOOSE QUESTION A OR QUESTION B)

WOULD YOU RATHER

USE A SEX TOY ON YOURSELF

 OR

ON YOUR PARTNER?

B

WOULD YOU RATHER

YOUR PARTNER GAVE YOU NICKNAMES DURING SEX

 OR

SCREAMED YOUR REAL NAME DURING SEX?

WOULD YOU RATHER ?
ADULT
VERSION

PLAYER 1

(ASK THE OTHER PLAYER(S) TO
CHOOSE QUESTION A OR QUESTION B)

A **WOULD YOU RATHER**

GET A BLOW JOB

 OR

A HANDJOB?

B **WOULD YOU RATHER**

HAVE YOUR FAMILY WATCH YOU HAVE SEX

 OR

YOUR NEIGHBORS?

WOULD YOU RATHER ?

ADULT
VERSION

PLAYER 2

(ASK THE OTHER PLAYER(S) TO
CHOOSE QUESTION A OR QUESTION B)

A = WOULD YOU RATHER

HAVE SEX WITH SOMEONE WHO NEVER SHOWERS

WITH SOMEONE WHO NEVER BRUSHES THEIR TEETH?

B = WOULD YOU RATHER

HAVE SEX WITH SOMEONE WHO DOESN'T MOVE

WHO DOESN'T MAKE ANY NOISE?

WOULD YOU RATHER ?
ADULT
VERSION

PLAYER 1

(ASK THE OTHER PLAYER(S) TO
CHOOSE QUESTION A OR QUESTION B)

A | WOULD YOU RATHER

HAVE SEX WITH SOMEONE WITH NO ARMS

OR

NO LEGS?

B | WOULD YOU RATHER

HAVE A THREESOME WITH TWO UGLY PEOPLE

OR

SEX WITH ONE SUPER HOT PERSON?

WOULD YOU RATHER ?

ADULT
VERSION

PLAYER 2

(ASK THE OTHER PLAYER(S) TO
CHOOSE QUESTION A OR QUESTION B)

A — WOULD YOU RATHER

HAVE SEX IN A CHURCH

 OR

IN YOUR PARENTS' BED?

B — WOULD YOU RATHER

BE A CHEAT

 OR

BE CHEATED ON?

WOULD YOU RATHER ?

ADULT
VERSION

PLAYER 1

(ASK THE OTHER PLAYER(S) TO
CHOOSE QUESTION A OR QUESTION B)

A =WOULD YOU RATHER=

HAVE SEX WITH A PORN STAR

 OR

A CELEBRITY?

B =WOULD YOU RATHER=

HAVE NUDES SHARED TO ALL YOUR FACEBOOK FRIENDS

 OR

TO YOUR GRANDPARENTS?

WOULD YOU RATHER ?

ADULT
VERSION

PLAYER 2

(ASK THE OTHER PLAYER(S) TO
CHOOSE QUESTION A OR QUESTION B)

A WOULD YOU RATHER

BE A SEX SLAVE

 OR

HAVE A SEX SLAVE?

B WOULD YOU RATHER

LAUGH

 OR

CRY DURING SEX?

WOULD YOU RATHER ?

ADULT
VERSION

PLAYER 1

(ASK THE OTHER PLAYER(S) TO
CHOOSE QUESTION A OR QUESTION B)

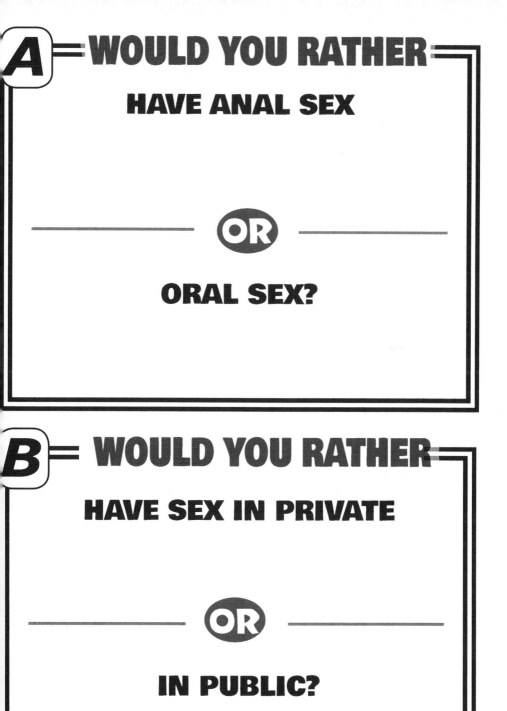

WOULD YOU RATHER ?

ADULT
VERSION

PLAYER 2

(ASK THE OTHER PLAYER(S) TO
CHOOSE QUESTION A OR QUESTION B)

A WOULD YOU RATHER

ACCIDENTALLY SHOUT AN EX'S NAME IN BED

 OR

SHOUT OUT "MOM!"

B WOULD YOU RATHER

NEVER GET TO HAVE SEX AGAIN

 OR

NEVER EAT SOLID FOOD AGAIN?

WOULD YOU RATHER ?

ADULT
VERSION

PLAYER 1

(ASK THE OTHER PLAYER(S) TO
CHOOSE QUESTION A OR QUESTION B)

WOULD YOU RATHER

HAVE AN ORGASM WHEN YOU SNEEZE

 OR

AN ORGASM WHEN YOU FART?

WOULD YOU RATHER

HAVE SEX WHILST HIGH

 OR

DRUNK SEX?

WOULD YOU RATHER ?
ADULT
VERSION

PLAYER 2

(ASK THE OTHER PLAYER(S) TO
CHOOSE QUESTION A OR QUESTION B)

A = WOULD YOU RATHER =

HAVE ORAL SEX BEFORE SLEEP

 OR

GET WOKEN UP WITH ORAL SEX?

B = WOULD YOU RATHER =

HAVE CHOCOLATE SAUCE LICKED OFF YOU

 OR

LICK CHOCOLATE SAUCE OF YOUR PARTNER ?

Made in the USA
Coppell, TX
31 March 2022

75788290R00057